11/2  11/3

SILVER
Silve  W9-ASP-241
218-226-4331

DO NOT INTERRUPT

# Do Not Interrupt

A Playful Take on the Art of Conversation

*Stephen Kuusisto*

WITHDRAWN

SILVER BAY PUBLIC LIBRARY

STERLING

New York / London
www.sterlingpublishing.com

For Marty Carver, Ed Stone, and Gary
Whittington, "symposiasts"

STERLING and the distinctive Sterling logo are registered
trademarks of Sterling Publishing Co., Inc.

10  9  8  7  6  5  4  3  2  1

Published by Sterling Publishing Co., Inc.
387 Park Avenue South, New York, NY 10016
© 2010 by Stephen Kuusisto
Distributed in Canada by Sterling Publishing
C/o Canadian Manda Group, 165 Dufferin Street,
Toronto, Ontario, Canada M6K 3H6

Manufactured in the United States of America
All rights reserved

Sterling ISBN 978-1-4027-6696-1
302.2 Kuu        OCLC  10/13/10
For information about custom editions, special sales,
premium and corporate purchases, please contact
Sterling Special Sales Department at 800-805-5489
or specialsales@sterlingpublishing.com.

# CONTENTS

# Prologue

*In times of joy, all of us wished
we possessed a tail we could wag.*

—W. H. Auden

**Two men in overcoats** sit in a garden in upstate New York in early spring. Snow has gone but the trees are not yet green. The thin oaks and birches have started to resound with birds.

The men are in their early thirties, both poetry professors at the local college, and they're wearing vintage fedoras and drinking champagne from paper cups. They are oblivious to their sooty lawn chairs and the lingering cold of early April.

The first man says, "I was green at birth, then suddenly I turned gold as a dancing shoe. And this afternoon I am happy with the moon rising in the east and feel I need nothing more. What a life I've had! What peculiar night blooming flowers are in my possession!"

The second says, "Mother dined out for years on the Indian railway station trick." He's alluding to his childhood in India. His mother would induce laughter from British colonial society by imitating all the sounds of an awakening rural railway station.

The first says, "I know a man in Helsinki who by day works as a respectable banker. His children go to the university; his wife writes for a leading newspaper. But that's only part of the story. On the weekends this man of business goes to the woods and talks to his personal rock. He has done this all his earthly life. Every man or woman in Finland finds his own woodland library if they're lucky."

"Did you ever climb a mountain with someone you love?" asks the second man. "No one who hasn't done this can fully understand the superior nature of bread and the touch of love's hand in the high altitudes."

In this way the two men share their respective anecdotes of joy until the sun goes down.

Oh yes, and they never interrupt each other.

DO NOT INTERRUPT

*one*

# The Principle of Simultaneous Elevations

**My first real conversation** was crazy. I'm guessing
that yours was too. Here's how it went:

> Me (four years old): "Why is the monkey
> in the cupboard?"
>
> Finnish Babysitter (forty-two years old):
> "Because the monkey was bad."
>
> Me: "Monkeys aren't bad!"
>
> Babysitter (I'll call her Kirsti): "Oh yes,
> the monkey was bad. He won't go to
> sleep."
>
> Me: "How can he sleep in a cupboard?"
>
> Kirsti: "Because he's got no one to talk to
> in there."
>
> Me: "He can talk to himself, you know!"
>
> Kirsti: "Go to bed!"
>
> Me: "I can hear the monkey talking in
> there!"
>
> Kirsti: "What's he saying?"
>
> Me: "He wants to go to the railroad
> station."
>
> Kirsti: "Why does he want to go to the
> railroad station?"
>
> Me: "Because he needs to go to the ice
> cream stand."

Conversation differs from talk.

Talkers are basically engaged in soliloquy. A talker generally doesn't notice that you exist.

A talker will only stop talking after you've expired and of course even this isn't certain.

I'm reminded of the slightly subversive and funny short story by Saki (H. H. Munro) in which "the husband" drones on and on to his wife about the empty nonsense of life and after many pages of monologue he finally stops talking and finds that his wife is dead in her armchair.

Yes, but as the Greeks well knew, people who are having a conversation are suddenly equals. We could call this the principle of "simultaneous elevations," for as the people converse they are experiencing mutually aroused curiosities. In my Helsinki flashback above, Kirsti realizes that our bedtime narrative about the stuffed monkey is turning into a little, unforeseeable mystery. Here's where it happened:

> Me: "I can hear the monkey talking in there!"

Kirsti: "What's he saying?"

Me: "He wants to go to the railroad station."

Kirsti: "Why does he want to go to the railroad station?"

Me: "Because he needs to go to the ice cream stand."

Strictly speaking a "conversation" is a moment of shared language marked by a mutually rewarding sense of surprise. "Poetry," said Ezra Pound, "is news that stays news." Pound was thinking of news less as dull journalism and more as surprise—a "news flash." Kirsti and I were sharing the news. Monkeys can be bad. Monkeys talk to themselves about railway kiosks.

How do you know when you've had a conversation instead of "a talk"?

Here's a good description of what happens when you've had a real conversation. This is from a letter written by Annie Sullivan, Helen Keller's famous teacher. Annie describes how her friend the inventor Alexander Graham Bell (who was a great benefactor of the deaf) could make her feel when they spoke together:

*I never felt at ease with anyone until I
met him. I was extremely conscious of my
crudeness. Dr. Bell had a happy way of
making people feel pleased with themselves.
After a conversation with him, I felt released,
important, communicative. All the pent-up
resentment within me went out . . .*

Conversationalists are always equal to their
partners, though the partners may not know this
as the conversation begins. This equalizing effect
is one of the shy, unasked-for prizes of sharing
our imaginations. The ancient Greeks called this
mutual engagement of minds a "symposium," which
essentially means "human beings in a state of
being connected." When Socrates and his friends
gathered their goal was to share their curiosity and
wonder about the mystery of being alive. News
that stays news.

As I've already remarked, conversation differs from talk. Talkers are generally interested in selling us something (a pathology, a polemic, or real estate, or deodorant liners for your sneakers). The talker loves cell phones, text messaging, and tweeting because these are media of assertion. Talkers are oddly Victorian: they think there's a right way and a wrong way to get through the hurried minutes. A talker is a perpetual adolescent. Just yesterday, a college girl sitting next to me on a bus sputtered into her mobile phone, "I can't believe she was wearing those pants—she's so fat!" Hearing her I was reminded that talkers assert themselves without evident curiosity: they talk from habit, their words securing them like cotton batting.

I imagined that girl was talking without any awareness that her listener was dead.

*two*

# Love's Body and Other Mysteries

**Human beings** often cannot anticipate when a conversation will start. Who after all can predict a surprise?

If you went to college in the United States before the end of the first Nixon administration, chances are good that you took a course called "Western Civ" and accordingly you read "the Greeks." I still remember a thin and severe professor of English standing before a packed auditorium and lecturing on the golden age of Athens. You may remember something similar.

One of the first things to catch my fancy way back then was the fact that the Greeks didn't trust the gods and goddesses any more than they trusted their neighbors. In effect, the Greeks looked to the heavens and saw that help was not guaranteed to be forthcoming.

Though I was only eighteen at the time I understood with raw clarity that the Greek pantheon wasn't flooded with light and that the notion of divine forgiveness wasn't up for discussion in the public square. I remember writing in the margin of a notebook: "Here and Now: A Big Deal!" The Greeks understood that life was a highly complicated layering of mysteries. Accordingly the quality of human engagement mattered far more than it seems to in the contemporary world.

Yes. For the Greeks, being conversant meant everything. Although the word *conversation* is Latinate, rather than Greek, the principle behind the word was wholly familiar to Plato. To be "conversant" was to share artful language or, as the Athenians would prefer to call it, to have "a dialectic"—an engagement of voices.

If you're a scholar—perhaps a philosopher or a rhetorician or a literary historian—you will most likely say that I'm simplifying things. One of my simplifications is a blending of imagination with dialectic. I am using the term *imagination* differently from the Greeks by substituting its modern meaning—what we've already described as Ezra Pound's sense of intellectual surprise. Plato and company would not have recognized this definition of imagination because the Hellenic philosophers distrusted poetry, believing it was a crude appeal to emotion. One can usefully compare Plato to those people who feared that the sight of Elvis Presley shaking his hips would ruin the lives of teenagers. In effect the Greeks thought that imagination was the lowest form of intelligence.

Yet Plato would easily agree, I think, that curiosity, dialogue, wonder, questioning, and mindful play are all representative of the highest intelligence. But for the sake of this little book I'm inserting our modernist view of imagination, which is less concerned with easy emotionality and more a characteristic of inquiry.

As noted, the Greeks saw that conversation could elevate several people at once and they called this kind of gathering a "symposium." (Of course you couldn't participate if you were a woman or a slave since in the "golden age" of Athens only men could be conversationalists.)

Still, despite its intellectual caste system, Plato's *Symposium* provides an entry into the art of conversation.

That art is very human. People converse because they're feeling good or bad. In the case of the *Symposium* the characters have hangovers.

Plato presents us with a group of dissipated men. As we say in the vernacular, "they're hungover" from a prior night's bout of wine drinking. This detail is what the American writer Tom Wolfe calls a "status-life" detail: a seemingly small thing that tells us a great deal about the characters. "This is a true story," Plato assures us. "Just look at these men."

Plato also tells us that this famous gathering of conversationalists has become the stuff of legend: the story is presented as a memory of a memory. In the opening passage Appollodorus recounts the history of the famous conversation to an unnamed companion. He says he heard the tale from Aristodemus, who was one of the participants in the actual conversation. The other participants represent a kind of Athenian VIP list: Phaedrus; Pausanias; Eryximachus; Aristophanes; Agathon; Socrates; Alcibiades; plus a troop of revelers.

The conversation is idiosyncratic. The participants propose to have a roundtable on the subject of love. Each man will speak love's praises.

Rule number one for a Greek conversation (and a good rule in our own time) is to sing the praises of your designated subject.

Praise meant more to the Greeks than the word commonly means in our times. Praise was both a description of merit but also of utility and cause. When praising love, Plato's gang will have to discuss what love is for and what it means. Try getting that on a Hallmark card.

The *Symposium* isn't a courtroom drama. It's not a debate. It's not a sermon made from call and response. No one is declared the winner. Playful talk is its own reward.

Who really knows what love is all about? No competent and honest soul can claim to understand this subject. It's the "monkey in the closet"— why is there something we call love?

Plato's philosophers are assiduous. "Let's talk about the importance and meaning of love," they say. "Let us surprise and elevate the entire group."

The first thing that has to happen in any good conversation is that someone has to break the ice, and in Greek terms that means being both speculative and amusing. The first to go is Eryximachus, who suggests that the gods of love haven't received as much praise from mankind as other gods and it's high time that men get going. He says, "Whereas other gods have poems and hymns made in their honor, the great and glorious god, Love, has no encomiast among all the poets who are so many."

(*Note*: whenever Plato uses the word *poet* he is employing it for comic effect. Plato held the poets in low esteem, believing they were intellectual lightweights. The amusing conceit that Eryximachus launches here is that love will now be praised by the most noble and discerning men in the land.)

Phaedrus is the first to praise love. He points out that love is the oldest of the gods and only chaos and the appearance of the earth are older. He then says (tongue in cheek) that love is the greatest benefactor to mankind for we are on our best behavior when we are in love. Phaedrus says that whole armies should be composed of lovers for no one would be a coward in the face of his beloved:

*For the principle, which ought to be the guide of men who would nobly live at principle, I say, neither kindred, nor honor, nor wealth, nor any other motive is able to implant so well as love. Of what am I speaking? Of the sense of honor and dishonor, without which neither states nor individuals ever do any good or great work. And I say that a lover who is detected in doing any dishonorable act, or submitting through cowardice when any dishonor is done to him by another, will be more pained at being detected by his beloved than at being seen by his father, or by his companions, or by any one else. The beloved too, when he is found in any disgraceful situation, has the same feeling about his lover. And if there were only some way of contriving that a state or an army should be made up of lovers and their loves, they would be the very best governors of their own city, abstaining from all dishonor, and emulating one another in honor; and when fighting at each other's side, although a mere handful, they would overcome the world. For what lover would not choose rather to be seen by all mankind*

*than by his beloved, either when abandoning*
*his post or throwing away his arms? He would*
*be ready to die a thousand deaths rather than*
*endure this. Or who would desert his beloved*
*or fail him in the hour of danger? The veriest*
*coward would become an inspired hero, equal*
*to the bravest, at such a time; Love would*
*inspire him. That courage which, as Homer*
*says, the god breathes into the souls of some*
*heroes, Love of his own nature infuses into*
*the lover.* [1]

Phaedrus is having fun. No one who engages
in warfare, which of course is the opposite
of love, would wish to look bad in the eyes of
his lover, hence that man would fight all the
harder. Remember that one of the primary aims
of Greek conversation was amusement. Exaggera-
tion and irony are essential when praising love.
If armies were made of lovers they would slaughter
more people.

Who can fault such logic?

Next comes Pausanias, who says that Phaedrus

---

[1]  From the online electronic edition of Plato's "Symposium,"
translated by Benjamin Jowett.

has neglected the fact that there are two kinds of love. Pausanias is erudite but humorless, pointing out that there are two Greek goddesses by the name of Aphrodite, one who is heavenly and one who represents common human lust. Pausanias says that we should all praise the higher form of love.

When Pausanias is done it's time for Aristophanes to speak but Plato tells us that he has the hiccoughs and he has to pass the baton to Eryximachus.

Eryximachus, who is a physician, tells Aristophanes:

*While I am speaking let me recommend you*
*to hold your breath, and if after you have done*
*so for some time the hiccough is no better,*
*then gargle with a little water; and if it still*
*continues, tickle your nose with something and*
*sneeze; and if you sneeze once or twice, even*
*the most violent hiccough is sure to go.*

This interlude serves as comic relief, coming as it does, after the rather dry and cheerless comments from Pausanias.

Eryximachus goes on to say that Pausanias is onto something with the idea that there are two kinds of love and that as a physician he can attest that there are also two kinds of love contained inside the bodies of all animals and men. He says:

> There are in the human body these two kinds
> of love, which are confessedly different and
> unlike, and being unlike, they have loves
> and desires which are unlike; and the desire
> of the healthy is one, and the desire of the
> diseased is another; and as Pausanias was
> just now saying that to indulge good men is
> honorable, and bad men dishonorable: so too
> in the body the good and healthy elements
> are to be indulged, and the bad elements
> and the elements of disease are not to be
> indulged, but discouraged. And this is what
> the physician has to do, and in this the art
> of medicine consists: for medicine may be
> regarded generally as the knowledge of the
> loves and desires of the body, and how to
> satisfy them or not; and the best physician
> is he who is able to separate fair love from
> foul, or to convert one into the other; and
> he who knows how to eradicate and how to
> implant love, whichever is required, and can
> reconcile the most hostile elements in the

*constitution and make them loving friends,*
*is a skillful practitioner.*

Eryximachus says the aim of the good physician is to form an understanding of the good love and the bad love residing inside the body and in turn bring these forces into harmony. He describes the art of medicine as being a kind of divination or alchemy. The dry and the wet, hot and cold, sweet and sour are brought into harmony by a good doctor. Harmony of the good and bad furnishes the highest form of love.

Aristophanes comes next and he notes that his hiccough is gone but he didn't get rid of it until he induced loud sneezing. He teases Eryximachus by saying, "I wonder whether the harmony of the body has a love of such noises and ticklings, for I no sooner applied the sneezing than I was cured."

Aristophanes next pronounces one of the most famous passages in Western literature by asserting that love has a complex history. At the dawn of time, he says, there were three kinds of beings: men, women, and a creature that was a unified man and woman—a being that the term *androgyny* can't adequately describe. He says:

*The sexes were not two as they are now, but originally three in number; there was man, woman, and the union of the two, having a name corresponding to this double nature, which had once a real existence, but is now lost, and the word "Androgynous" is only preserved as a term of reproach. In the second place, the primeval man was round, his back and sides forming a circle; and he had four hands and four feet, one head with two faces, looking opposite ways, set on a round neck and precisely alike; also four ears, two privy members, and the remainder to correspond. He could walk upright as men now do, backward or forward as he pleased, and he could also roll over and over at a great pace, turning on his four hands and four feet, eight in all, like tumblers going over and over with their legs in the air; this was when he wanted to run fast.*

Aristophanes goes on to develop a mythological description of a war between humankind and the gods, a story he unfolds in the service of understanding and praising love. His story is so inventive

I'm quoting it in its entirety:

*At last, after a good deal of reflection, Zeus discovered a way. He said: "Methinks I have a plan which will humble their pride and improve their manners; men shall continue to exist, but I will cut them in two and then they will be diminished in strength and increased in numbers; this will have the advantage of making them more profitable to us. They shall walk upright on two legs, and if they continue insolent and will not be quiet, I will split them again and they shall hop about on a single leg." He spoke and cut men in two, like a sorb-apple which is halved for pickling, or as you might divide an egg with a hair; and as he cut them one after another, he bade Apollo give the face and the half of the neck a turn in order that the man might contemplate the section of himself: he would thus learn a lesson of humility. Apollo was also bidden to heal their wounds and compose their forms. So he gave a turn to the face and pulled the skin from the sides all over that which in our language is called the belly, like the purses*

which draw in, and he made one mouth at the
center, which he fastened in a knot (the same
which is called the navel); he also molded
the breast and took out most of the wrinkles,
much as a shoemaker might smooth leather
upon a last; he left a few, however, in the
region of the belly and navel, as a memorial
of the primeval state. After the division the
two parts of man, each desiring his other half,
came together, and throwing their arms about
one another, entwined in mutual embraces,
longing to grow into one, they were on the
point of dying from hunger and self-neglect,
because they did not like to do anything apart;
and when one of the halves died and the other
survived, the survivor sought another mate,
man or woman as we call them, being the
sections of entire men or women, and clung
to that. They were being destroyed, when
Zeus in pity of them invented a new plan:
he turned the parts of generation round to
the front, for this had not been always their
position and they sowed the seed no longer as
hitherto like grasshoppers in the ground, but
in one another; and after the transposition

*the male generated in the female in order
that by the mutual embraces of man and
woman they might breed, and the race might
continue; or if man came to man they might
be satisfied, and rest, and go their ways to the
business of life: so ancient is the desire of one
another which is implanted in us, reuniting
our original nature, making one of two, and
healing the state of man.*

*Each of us when separated, having
one side only, like a flat fish, is but the
indenture of a man, and he is always looking
for his other half. Men who are a section of
that double nature which was once called
Androgynous are lovers of women; adulterers
are generally of this breed, and also adulterous
women who lust after men: the women who
are a section of the woman do not care for
men, but have female attachments; the female
companions are of this sort. But they who
are a section of the male follow the male,
and while they are young, being slices of
the original man, they hang about men and
embrace them, and they are themselves the
best of boys and youths, because they have the*

*most manly nature. Some indeed assert that
they are shameless, but this is not true; for
they do not act thus from any want of shame,
but because they are valiant and manly, and
have a manly countenance, and they embrace
that which is like them. And these when they
grow up become our statesmen, and these
only, which is a great proof of the truth of
what I am saving. When they reach manhood
they are loves of youth, and are not naturally
inclined to marry or beget children, if at all,
they do so only in obedience to the law; but
they are satisfied if they may be allowed to
live with one another unwedded; and such
a nature is prone to love and ready to return
love, always embracing that which is akin to
him. And when one of them meets with his
other half, the actual half of himself, whether
he be a lover of youth or a lover of another
sort, the pair are lost in an amazement of love
and friendship and intimacy, and would not
be out of the other's sight, as I may say, even
for a moment: these are the people who pass
their whole lives together; yet they could not
explain what they desire of one another. For*

*the intense yearning which each of them has toward the other does not appear to be the desire of lover's intercourse, but of something else which the soul of either evidently desires and cannot tell, and of which she has only a dark and doubtful presentiment. Suppose Hephaestus, with his instruments, to come to the pair who are lying side by side and to say to them, "What do you people want of one another?"—they would be unable to explain. And suppose further, that when he saw their perplexity he said: "Do you desire to be wholly one; always day and night to be in one another's company? For if this is what you desire, I am ready to melt you into one and let you grow together, so that being two you shall become one, and while you live a common life as if you were a single man, and after your death in the world below still be one departed soul instead of two—I ask whether this is what you lovingly desire, and whether you are satisfied to attain this?"—there is not a man of them who when he heard the proposal would deny or would not acknowledge that this meeting and melting into one another, this becoming one instead of two, was the very expression of his ancient need. And the reason is that human nature was originally one and we were a whole, and the desire and pursuit of the whole is called love. There was a time, I say, when we were one, but now because of the wickedness of mankind God has dispersed us, as the Arcadians were dispersed into villages by the Lacedaemonians. And if we are not obedient to the gods, there is a danger that we shall be split up again and go about in basso-relievo, like the profile figures having only half a nose which are sculptured on monuments, and that we shall be like tallies.*

*Wherefore let us exhort all men to piety, that we may avoid evil, and obtain the good, of which Love is to us the lord and minister; and let no one oppose him—he is the enemy of the gods who oppose him. For if we are friends of the God and at peace with him we shall find our own true loves, which rarely happens in this world at present. I am serious, and therefore I must beg Eryximachus not to make fun or to find any allusion in what I am saying to Pausanias and Agathon, who, as*

*I suspect, are both of the manly nature, and belong to the class that I have been describing. But my words have a wider application—they include men and women everywhere; and I believe that if our loves were perfectly accomplished, and each one returning to his primeval nature had his original true love, then our race would be happy. And if this would be best of all, the best in the next degree and under present circumstances must be the nearest approach to such a union; and that will be the attainment of a congenial love. Wherefore, if we would praise him who has given to us the benefit, we must praise the god Love, who is our greatest benefactor, both leading us in this life back to our own nature, and giving us high hopes for the future, for he promises that if we are pious, he will restore us to our original state, and heal us and make us happy and blessed. This, Eryximachus, is my discourse of love, which, although different to yours, I must beg you to leave unassailed by the shafts of your ridicule, in order that each may have his turn; each, or rather either, for Agathon and Socrates are the only ones left.*

There is much that is noble in Aristophanes's story. The yearnings of men for women or the yearnings of same sex couples are explained as coefficients of a primeval human war with the gods, and Aristophanes's explanation holds no form of yearning to be superior. All humankind is lonely for its lost halves. We are all in bereavement for our former state. No one can explain the depth of our emotions or the nature of our longings. We are homesick for our ancient bodies and our first loves. In our ancient and undivided condition we were happy and blessed. That is the highest condition of love.

Remember that the aim of the symposium is to have a simultaneous experience of elevation. We are admitting ideas in a mutual conversant dance of surprises. Aristophanes is aware that he has told a strange and beautiful story, a story that's wholly improbable, as improbable as love itself. He knows his story is vaguely silly but he reminds his friends to withhold their amusement until the remaining participants have had their say. "Don't break the spell" he seems to be saying. Though his story is a tall tale, even by Greek standards, Aristophanes has raised the ante—he's decided to explain what our yearnings are for.

Agathon is the next to speak. He has the unenviable position of having to make his praises of love before Socrates. This is like having to sing before Caruso or Pavarotti. No sane man would give it a try.

Agathon's premise is that love is the youngest of the gods and that young people are therefore the greatest followers of love. He argues for the tenderness of love. He sounds a little bit like a late-sixties, "love power" hippie proclaiming that love never visits those who are not soft in their souls and that the wisdom of love is its own powerful society. He concludes:

> *Therefore, Phaedrus, I say of Love that he is the fairest and best in himself, and the cause of what is fairest and best in all other things. And there comes into my mind a line of poetry in which he is said to be the god who*
> *Gives peace on earth and calms the stormy deep,*
> *Who stills the winds and bids the sufferer sleep.*
> *This is he who empties men of disaffection and fills them with affection, who makes them to meet together at banquets*

*such as these: in sacrifices, feasts, dances, he
is our lord—who sends courtesy and sends
away discourtesy, who gives kindness ever and
never gives unkindness; the friend of the good,
the wonder of the wise, the amazement of the
gods; desired by those who have no part in
him, and precious to those who have the better
part in him; parent of delicacy, luxury, desire,
fondness, softness, grace; regardful of the good,
regardless of the evil: in every word, work,
wish, fear-savior, pilot, comrade, helper; glory
of gods and men, leader best and brightest: in
whose footsteps let every man follow, sweetly
singing in his honor and joining in that sweet
strain with which love charms the souls of
gods and men. Such is the speech, Phaedrus,
half-playful, yet having a certain measure of
seriousness, which, according to my ability, I
dedicate to the god.*

Agathon is arguing that love is its own just
reward and that its gods are the lovers of those
who love, and indifferent to those who possess
any kind of evil in their hearts. He sounds like the
Beatles: "All you need is love, love. Love is all you

need." Finally Plato tells us that everyone cheers as Agathon concludes.

Now as we've said already Socrates is the last of our conversationalists. He starts by saying that he's not the man to praise love as the others have done, but he will instead tell the truth about love. (Talk about raising the ante!) For a brief moment he sounds like an ancient Greek version of Jack Nicholson, since he asks rhetorically if the assembly wants to know the truth where love is concerned. Of course they all assent. Again it's important to remember that this conversation is designed to be an exercise in group elevation. Who would walk out before Socrates had a chance to speak?

If, as I suggested earlier, you went to college in the era of "Western Civ," you will remember that Socrates is the greatest questioner in all of history. He decides to interrogate poor Agathon by asking him to confirm or deny a series of propositions about yearning. Socrates is looking for contradictions in Agathon's view that love is basically sufficient unto itself. Even after twenty-five hundred years have elapsed we can hear that Socrates is having a little fun at Agathon's expense. Here's how he begins:

*Remember further what you said in your
speech, or if you do not remember I will
remind you: you said that the love of the
beautiful set in order the empire of the gods,
for that of deformed things there is no love—
did you not say something of that kind?*

*Yes, said Agathon.*

*Yes, my friend, and the remark was a just
one. And if this is true, Love is the love of
beauty and not of deformity?*

*He assented.*

*And the admission has been already
made that Love is of something which a man
wants and has not?*

*True, he said.*

*Then Love wants and has not beauty?*

*Certainly, he replied.*

*And would you call that beautiful which
wants and does not possess Beauty?*

*Certainly not.*

*Then would you still say that love is
beautiful?*

*Agathon replied: I fear that I did not
understand what I was saying.*

Socrates then tells an inventive story about how the gods who are composed of love escape the human condition of wanting or hoping for love—that is, he explains that mortals understand the higher love of the gods, but cannot wholly achieve it. Humans can have an experience or forethought of divine love, but not the same love that defines the lives of the gods. Our prayers for love must reach the gods through an intermediate spirit, called a daemon. Our lives must be dedicated to the ardor and desire for higher love, though we cannot perforce know what the gods know.

This brings the symposium to an end. By telling an inventive tale that delights as well as instructs, Socrates proves the twin imperatives of Greek story-telling. Love must be our hope in this life but also of the spirit: mystic, unseen at first, all embracing, larger than corporality—"a love supreme"—as John Coltrane would call it some three thousand years later. Socrates favors the soul. He says in effect that men should avoid shallow fascinations in the name of love. When we do this we praise the divine and live in accord with true love.

It's interesting to see how Socrates conveys his part of the conversation by using a story. He invites his listeners into a remembrance of a conversation he once had with a wise woman, and he gives them room to join in the direction of his narrative concerning love's morality. He is conscious that the goal of conversation is to elevate and delight each of its participants.

I have spent some time with the *Symposium* because it's the first genuine conversation we have in Western literature and it offers those who admire conversation a true model of imaginative language shared and promoted, without the contemporary preoccupation with selling an idea or crowning winners and deriding losers. The *Symposium* is not a debate. It isn't a polemical or liturgical event. Instead it's a round table of imaginations and that, as they say, is the ticket.

When it comes to the art of conversation, the Greeks had a major advantage over modern people because they actually needed to have discourse around their tables or in the public square. The demand for intellectual and imaginative play rendered in spoken language has disappeared from our world, though that disappearance is a comparatively recent historical development. Conversation for the sake of pleasure was widely practiced in the eighteenth century and even well into the nineteenth century.

We can suggest that the furious pace of the industrial revolution, with its new workaday model of labor over leisure, may have contributed to the decline of true conversation. It's possible that the rise of modern newspapers and the consequent rise of electronic media added to the erosion of the art of mutual elevation and play. But these are only what we might call cultural tendencies, like the disappearance of the piano in the parlor and the family "sing-along" that once constituted the mainstay of neighborly entertainments.

The truth is we can have conversations again. And we can enjoy them in much the way Socrates did.

*three*

# A Symposium Remembered after Twenty Years

**Here is a real life** symposium I'm remembering after many years. Because I can no longer recall the exact words spoken on the night in question, I'm changing the names of my fellow Greeks. The gist or tenor of what we said is in the province of truth.

It was late spring at a small college by a lake. The flowering trees were suddenly little factories of joys we hadn't remembered to ask for. Winter does that. It takes away parts of one's hope, though it does it so slowly you'll never sense your individual losses. I was walking in the twilight with three splendid friends—all of them were poets and the tiny fingers of night were pushing each of us along, as if reminding us we'd been asleep and should make up for it. In turn we were trading bits of poetry. "Do you remember this one?" I asked. "It's by Antonio Machado: 'Music! A naked woman runs mad through the pure night!'"

One of my friends (who I'll call Joseph) said, "The men in the white coats chase naked music disguised as a madwoman through the night. Boy, poetry can lose its flavor pretty quickly."

My other friend (who I'll call Henry) said, "The men in the white coats are stunned by the naked music and forget the ascendant madwoman who becomes a laurel tree."

"Oh," I said, "if madwomen live inside trees then I say they don't live in the laurel, they live in the locust."

My third friend Sean said simply, "I think the locust tree is the dirtiest damned tree. I hope there's a better fate for abstract madwomen than to live there."

We were happy and walking to the home of friends, where we would have a fine dinner and more than a little wine, and where we would talk about anything at all. The anticipatory pleasure of free talk—real talk—is a wonderful thing. We knew we would have the sort of conversation that comes from mutual happiness, that's as lovely as the trees and the nearly full moon, and the first instance of spring dusk when the day's heat doesn't vanish but lingers awhile.

We arrived at the home of our friend, whom I will call Diotima, in honor of the woman who inspired Socrates. Diotima was an administrator at the local college, a scholar of French literature, a Jewish survivor of the German occupation of her Eastern European homeland, and a lovely organizer of informal symposia.

With Diotima was her paramour, whom I'll call Gunnar. Gunnar was a retired sailor from the merchant marine and the kind of man who can explain why the clocks run faster in mad King Ludwig's castle, or why the East River in New York City flows quicker than the Hudson, though this shouldn't be the case.

We were the kind of people who didn't talk about office politics or who might be cheating on his or her spouse. It's not that we were above that sort of thing. It's simply the case that we loved having our own symposia. We all understood from our respective struggles with life that inventive dialogue was the "real ticket," as they say in New York. As I look back on it now I imagine we discovered this by accident. We must have gotten together one evening and straightaway we talked about the Egyptian idea of time as a component in architecture. We were hooked.

Joseph was reading a book about mysticism. He was wildly in love with anything having to do with spiritual life. He was a natural minister, though he had no church. He resembled the young Oscar Wilde and this was no accident. He was British, beautiful, thin, and gay, and in love with gods and goddesses.

Sean was a non-believer. He was raised a working-class, Catholic kid in Pennsylvania. He'd spent the rest of his life sharpening his skepticism about religion, and even though he was a professor in the humanities, he read about science with avidity and appreciation.

Henry was from New York City. He grew up just a stone's throw from Yankee Stadium. He knew more about the literature of human suffering and comic irony than anyone I'd ever met. That's the way it is with people who are street smart first and book smart second. He's still the best-read guy I know.

We drank Merlot and picked at olives and finger foods and I mentioned the moon, which was almost full. I said that sometimes the moon is so bright it makes me feel both thrilled and lonely. I quoted (wrongly) some lines from the Spanish poet Federico García Lorca: "When the full moon rises dark waters cover the earth and the heart feels it is a little island in the infinite."

Joseph observed that there is no need to feel lonely. "Everything is connected in God's universe," he said.

"To see a world in a grain of sand, And a heaven in a wildflower, Hold infinity in the palm of your hand, And eternity in an hour," I said, quoting William Blake.

"Yes," said Gunnar, who had just walked into the room. "But Blake's lines only tell of God's presence in things and they don't address the loneliness."

Sean raised his glass. "It was the great mystic Orson Welles who said, 'We're born alone, we live alone, we die alone. Only through our love and friendship can we create the illusion for the moment that we're not alone.'"

"I think that would make Welles an anti-mystic," said Henry. "Anyway," he continued, "the issue of loneliness has to do with a state of mind. Being lonely and being in solitude is not the same thing. And that's not just semantics. Solitude is an active mental operation. The Lorca lines and the Blake lines are active states of mind."

We were starting to have some fun. We didn't have to appoint a winner. We were talking about God and solitude and beauty in a small house in upstate New York. I wondered whether there might be a similar group holding its own symposium on the far side of the lake in one of those houses that shines out there in the dark.

Diotima asked, "Do you mean that if you choose to be alone then one doesn't feel lonely?" Her bracelets tinkled as she put a lit candle on the table.

Joseph replied: "Everyone is lonely. People who believe in God are lonely. The difference between a religious loneliness and that of Orson Welles is that religious belief retains our human and ancient sense of wonder, and wonder is intuitively secure. Paul Tillich said, 'Being religious means asking passionately the question of the meaning of our existence and being willing to receive answers even if the answers hurt.'"

"You've got me," said Sean. "I walked out of the Catholic Church as soon as I was out of short pants. Belief is painful; non-belief is painful; the only thing we know for sure is the scientific method. Science proves things. Religion asserts unprovable feelings. If I have to be lonely I'd rather be with the scientists; at least they're not hooked on superstitions. I mean, what does that mean—being willing to receive answers? Is God some kind of radio? Science finds answers."

Joseph was clearly happy. You could actually feel his pleasure. He didn't really care if he converted Sean to a religious view. This was the unstated thing. No one would have to be the victor. I said that the question of belief is similar for religion and science—that in effect every moment in life is driven by the wish that our hopes will be satisfied.

We agreed that science tests propositions and that religion makes the untestable claim that belief is its own reward.

We agreed that loneliness is deep in our very tissues.

Someone said that miracles and scientific discoveries are both unforeseeable.

Sean pointed out that you can test scientific discoveries but you can only make unproven claims for a religious point of view.

Diotima mentioned that it's possible lonely people are more disposed to a belief in God, while introspective people might be more disposed to the laboratory.

I suggested that plenty of scientists believe in God, but they trust also in experiments. I joked that there seemed to be very few scientists among Jesus's disciples.

Someone pointed out that Jesus said nothing

about curiosity or intellectual inquiry, but asserted instead that "Blessed are the poor in spirit, for theirs is the kingdom of heaven."

"So the thing is that religion asks us to believe in what we cannot see," Sean said. Then he added, "Why then does Jesus cure so many blind people?"

"Blindness is a metaphor for lack of knowledge," I said. "But it was also one of the commonest disabilities in the ancient world, owing to things like scarlet fever."

"So Jesus has it both ways?" Sean asked.

"Yes," I said. "Jesus cures the blind and they are thereby walking signs of the miraculous. On the other hand, don't we want to do the same thing? Let's cure diseases. We need science to do that."

We agreed that loneliness is probably not curable by scientific means.

Joseph, ever amused, argued that God was in his salad and that God was also in Sean's salad if he would just bother to taste it.

Sean said he thought he was tasting lemon juice.

Someone then quoted from Monty Python:

*All things dull and ugly,*
*all creatures short and squat.*
*All things rude and nasty,*
*the Lord God made the lot.*

Gunnar proposed that God made the lemon so we could eat the grasshopper and the tarantula.

We were of course just a little drunk by that time.

We argued about holy men and women and we talked about the Enlightenment, and because we liked one another, and owing to the wine and the moon, we felt what the Greeks felt: a contentment arising from our shared passion for life. Not one of us could say beyond ardor what this meant. We knew that meaning is still a mystery. We knew that talking beats watching TV.

*four*

# Free and Easy

*After the exercises which the health*
*of the body requires, and which have*
*themselves a natural tendency to actuate*
*and invigorate the mind, the most eligible*
*amusement of a rational being seems to*
*be that interchange of thoughts which is*
*practised in free and easy conversation;*
*where suspicion is banished by experience,*
*and emulation by benevolence; where every*
*man speaks with no other restraint than*
*unwillingness to offend, and hears with no*
*other disposition than desire to be pleased.*

—Samuel Johnson: Rambler
#89 (January 22, 1751)

**When I think** of Samuel Johnson's words above and in particular the phrase "where suspicion is banished by experience, and emulation by benevolence; where every man speaks with no other restraint than unwillingness to offend, and hears with no other disposition than desire to be pleased," I remember an early conversation with my father.

Back when I was about eight years old my dad gave me a hatchet and, like any sensible eight-year-old boy, I went out in the backyard and methodically cut down a newly planted, decorative fruit tree, which of course took a long time since it was still green under the bark. When my dad confronted me about the matter I said, "I'm no George Washington. Hoodlums stole my hatchet!" This of course became a family slogan of sorts. When my mother backed our station wagon into a parked oil truck she simply told my dad that hoodlums stole the car. When my younger sister got caught smoking cigarettes in junior high, it was hoodlums who made her do it. As near as I can recall, my conversation with my father went something like this:

Me: "I am not George Washington.
     Hoodlums cut down this tree."
Father: "Really? My word! Whatever did
     they look like?"
Me: "They were wrapped in onion-skin
     typing paper but I don't know why."
Father: "Were they tall or short, thin or
     fat? Maybe we can send out a posse."
Me: "Thin. They were trying to look big
     with all that typing paper. I think
     they were hungry hoodlums."

Father: "But if they were hungry why cut
    down a sapling without fruit?"
Me: "I think they were planning to eat
    the leaves."

I was lucky in that instance that my father recognized that I was essentially without fault. He'd
given me the hatchet without providing accompa-
nying rules. In turn I used the thing in the time-
honored way. The lovely thing about my childhood
was that I grew up among conversationalists. I had
them on both sides of the family: my dad was a Finn,
who had grown up in a culture of "sauna talk," and
my mom was from a salty, colorful Boston-Irish
family. Dr. Johnson's notion that conversation is
built from a mutual desire not to offend, and that
it's based on the delivery of respective pleasure, is
what we practiced.

Don't get me wrong. We could be rather silly if
the occasion called for it. But we tried not to hurt

anyone. My mother once had the following conversation with a traveling Bible salesman. (I know
because I was home from school feigning illness
and so I heard the whole thing.)

> Salesman: "Hello, Madame. It is my
> privilege today to make you a gift of
> the good word with this handsome
> edition of the Holy Bible and this
> offer is absolutely free!"

> Mother: "A free Bible! Well land sakes! I
> was just now thinking to myself how
> nice it would be to curl up with a
> comforting book!"

> Salesman: "There's no comfort like
> the Good Book! We're pleased at
> the Amalgamated Synoptic Gospel
> Benevolence Society to offer you this
> leather-tooled volume complete with
> pinked pages topped off with faux
> gold leaf for absolutely free!"

> Mother: "Now, now. You and I both
> know that nothing's free. Why even
> John the Baptist had to pay for his
> locusts and honey."

> Salesman: "He did?"

Mother: "Yes my dear, you see honey
and locusts don't occur naturally
side by side and someone had to put
them together for John, much the
way you'd make a peanut butter and
jelly sandwich. The bearer of honey-
dipped locusts was therefore either
a slave or else he got paid. I prefer to
think that he got paid, don't you?"

Salesman: "I'm sure that John the
Baptist paid for his locusts. He had
to have been an honorable man. Say,
can I have a glass of water?"

She let the salesman into the kitchen. This
was in the autumn of 1964. Shortly thereafter
my mother would read Truman Capote's *In Cold
Blood* and that would be the end of inviting stray
salesmen into the house. She gave him his glass of
water. Then she resumed:

"Did you know that John the Baptist wore a
shirt made from camel skin?"

"No," said the salesman, who peered doubtfully
into his glass.

"Oh yes, he is described as wearing strange gar-
ments in the wilderness and that means camel.

City dwellers might have worn woven robes but in the desert you would have to wear camel hide."

"Boy," said the salesman, "I bet that must have been hot and itchy."

"Oh yes, you can't wear a skin without scratching. That's why John went into the water you see."

"Really?" The salesman was suddenly alert.

"Yes," my mother said. "He went straight into the water, skin and all. That way it would stay cool as he wandered the wilderness with Christ's future disciples, Andrew and Peter. I'm pretty certain that they wore skins too."

"Well I confess I've never thought about this before," said the salesman. "Of course this makes sense. Camel skins. My word!" He looked at my mother as if he were seeing her for the first time.

"You know," he said, "camels have semi-transparent eyelids, which means they can shut their eyes in a sandstorm and still see where they're going. I think that makes them kind of magical, don't you?"

My mother was practicing what Dr. Johnson called the desire not to offend and she was doing this with pleasure. The salesman departed shortly thereafter and it's safe to surmise that after meeting my mother he never thought about John the Baptist in quite the same way.

The art of conversation can be a kind of tomfoolery—a bit of "having us on," as they say in Britain, but the feckless and adolescent business of demeaning your interlocutor is altogether forbidden. The example above demonstrates that it's possible to confound your fellow conversant and still remain agreeable. Socrates wouldn't have had it any other way.

*five*

# Talking to Yourself

*Most of us who turn to any subject we love*
*remember some morning or evening hour*
*when we got on a high stool to reach down*
*an untried volume, or sat with parted lips*
*listening to a new talker, or for very lack of*
*books began to listen to the voices within,*
*as the first traceable beginning of our love.*

—T. S. Eliot

**Sometimes whether** we like it or not we're forced to talk to ourselves. To the best of my knowledge no one has written a primer on this subject. Occasionally there's a movie like *Castaway*, starring Tom Hanks, in which a marooned character must keep up a conversation with the various parts of his psyche.

One doesn't have to be in a gothic and far-away location to talk with your inner life. In fact, the practice we gain by doing this is one heck of a skill.

My grandmother once shook Richard Nixon's hand as she stood outside a leather tannery in Peabody, Massachusetts. The next thing we knew she stopped using the hand, refused to wash it, carried it about on an invisible pillow. In effect, her hand became what philosophers call "an independent object," like a flame in dry flowers.

My grandmother was a Finnish minister's wife. She was devout and introspective and she didn't really talk to her hand, but I want to illustrate how one can have a complete and rather delightful conversation, as she might have done. Here's how it would go:

Grandmother (alone in parsonage, talking to her right hand): "I think today was my lucky day. But I generally see purposes and intentions in everything. Of course I wouldn't tell my neighbors, but I believe in magic and I have a lucky rabbit's foot in my purse."

The Nixon Hand: "I believe in crises, conspiracies; I abjure the childish anthropomorphism that puts God inside a cloud or in the eyes of dogs."

Grandmother: "Oh, oh, oh! Dogs are filthy! I don't care what anyone says, they don't have souls!"

The Nixon Hand: "But you would agree that there are lucky dogs?"

Grandmother: "Dogs can't go to heaven!"

The Nixon Hand: "Look, excuse me, I
don't know how to say this, you look
like a nice lady, but we have real
enemies!"

Grandmother: "Don't you tell me about
enemies: when the Russians drop
spoons in the snow they can hear it in
Helsinki, which means they hear it in
Duluth!"

The Hand: "Jesus! I should have known
Khrushchev didn't have any spoons!
What else do they say in Duluth!?"

Grandmother: "They don't say anything.
Quiet people, Finns and Norwegians.
It's dryly cold. You can hear the
hinges on the mailboxes."

The Hand: "Don't give me that!
Everyone's got funny little debts!
Everyone flaps against the hedges.
Or goes alone to the county fair and
looks up at the rising lights of the
Ferris wheel and says something
aloud, something jaundiced tossed
out at children or strangers . . .

Grandmother: "God provides. All you
    need to do is step gingerly over the
    fallen trees."

I am of course having some fun here at my
grandmother's expense and may all my blessed
relatives in heaven forgive me. But I can't resist
sharing this tiny dramatic dialogue between my
grandmother and her possessed hand.

It is a fact that conversation can be conducted
inside your head. Remember the goal of all conversation is to achieve the simultaneous art of elevation. In this imaginary talk my grandmother and
the Nixon hand are each amused in their characteristic ways. The next time you're on a long trip
in a car by yourself or you're stuck in an airport
without a book, just give this exercise a try. Before
I return to the subject of conversing with others
I just need to add that when you play the game
above (which I like to call "2 H" for "Hand and

History") it's useful to pick an odd figure from history and an equally eccentric person with whom you are directly acquainted. There are no other rules for this game. Be as brief or as long as you like. You may write the results in a notebook or let your amusements evanesce, like all the other unreported conversations of history.

# six

# Having a Party with Thomas Aquinas

**In the late Middle Ages** Thomas Aquinas sought to debate the role of God in nature by reintroducing Aristotle's use of syllogism. Syllogism, as we all remember, is the form of deductive reasoning that incorporates a general statement, a second more precise statement, and a third concluding statement, which is drawn from the others.

Here is the most recognizable example:

*All men are mortal.*
*Socrates is a man.*
*Socrates is mortal.*

We can play with this:

*Socrates is mortal.*
*Cows are mortal.*
*Socrates is a cow.*

Playing with syllogisms is a terrific way to start a symposium at home or in a submarine for that matter. Here are a few useful tips:

Use syllogisms as a way to extend the delight factor of your symposium.

Start with the word *all* since it inevitably creates logical or illogical conditions.

> *All planets revolve.*
> *My Uncle Vinnie revolves when he's had a six-pack.*
> *When he's had a six-pack my Uncle Vinnie is a planet.*

> *All planets named Uncle Vinnie are intoxicated.*
> *All drunks see drunk planets.*
> *Astronomers are drunks.*

After a while playing with syllogism will inevitably become too patterned. At this point it can be fun to take the nouns and make them the subjects of their own symposium.

> *Sing the praises of drunk planets and their gods.*
> *Sing the praises of sober planets and their gods.*
> *Musical planets; planets without borders. A planet that is ruled by animals and their gods.*

Rinse and repeat.

*seven*

# Times of Joy

**Rebecca West** once wrote, "There is not such a thing as conversation. It is an illusion. There are only intersecting monologues."

Nothing could be further from the truth.

It is true that conversation doesn't occur naturally around a dinner table. Ordinary gossip or egocentric grandstanding will not furnish the ingredients for a symposium.

As I've suggested in chapter 2, if one wants to have a conversation there has to be agreement that playful talk will be the shared order of business.

A friend of mine, who attended Christ Church College at Oxford, once had me in stitches relating how the old dons would sit together in the dining hall, huddled at high table, far from the faculty and students. He described their genteel shabbiness, their food-stained neckties, their tweed coats. Then he related their conversation. It seems that the weathered old academics liked to drink claret and share their respective observations about its flavor. According to my friend the conversation went something like this:

> Don #1: "Rather a bosky, dark slant on
>      the tongue . . ."
>
> Don #2: "Well, maybe a dark forest but

I think it's more of Lake Lentini in Sicily, there's something of minty reeds, don't you think?"

Don #3: Well I don't know. I think it's more a burlesque: the tannins are a bit ragged like a clown pulling at his threads."

Don #4: "I taste something Rosicrucian and plangent."

Don #5: "No, no, all of you! This is the flavor of a mossy stone, a stone that the light reaches but once a day and for one hour only. I shall call this inestimable claret the tears of Sarah, for one must be very old and should be in childbirth to drink it."

The masters of conversation are *everywhere* and yet we must seek them out. Genial talkers are democratic with a small *d*—they prefer conversing to establishing the superiority of their causes. They are the best of friends or new acquaintances. And when we don't have them before us in the flesh we can find them in the arts.

In literature there may be no more celebrated conversationalist than Samuel Johnson, who among other things, was the first person to compile an English language dictionary. If you were the first person to write a dictionary, wouldn't you most likely want to get out occasionally and talk to people? We know about Dr. Johnson's delight in conversation because his friend James Boswell wrote *The Life of Johnson*, one of the classic biographies in English literature. One can find lively conversation recorded throughout the book.

Dr. Johnson was the kind of conversationalist whom the Roman orator Cicero would have admired. Cicero famously established some rules for good conversation, which included:

* Speak clearly.

* Speak easily, but not too much, give others their turn.

* Do not interrupt.

- ❖ Be courteous.

- ❖ Deal seriously with serious matters, gracefully with lighter ones.

- ❖ Never criticize people behind their backs.

- ❖ Stick to subjects of general interest.

- ❖ Do not talk about yourself.

- ❖ Never lose your temper.

In *The Life of Johnson*, James Boswell relates how Dr. Johnson was approached on the street by a man whom he hadn't seen for more than forty years. The passage is lovely since it illustrates Johnson's willingness to have a true conversation with someone he scarcely knows. The passage also demonstrates that Johnson was more interested in conversing than with categorizing or rating the intellectual pedigree of his fellow talker, a matter that's of keen importance, if one truly wants to converse. Here's what Boswell tells us:

> *And now I am to give a pretty full account of one of the most curious incidents in Johnson's life, of which he himself has made the*

*following minute on this day: 'In my return
from church, I was accosted by Edwards,
an old fellow-collegian, who had not seen
me since 1729. He knew me, and asked if I
remembered one Edwards; I did not at first
recollect the name, but gradually as we walked
along, recovered it, and told him a conversation
that had passed at an alehouse between us. My
purpose is to continue our acquaintance.'*

*It was in Butcher-row that this meeting
happened. Mr. Edwards, who was a decent-
looking elderly man in grey clothes, and a
wig of many curls, accosted Johnson with
familiar confidence, knowing who he was,
while Johnson returned his salutation with
a courteous formality, as to a stranger. But as
soon as Edwards had brought to his recollection
their having been at Pembroke-College together
nine-and-forty years ago, he seemed much
pleased, asked where he lived, and said he
should be glad to see him in Bolt-court.*

*EDWARDS. 'Ah, Sir! we are old men now.'*

*JOHNSON. (Who never liked to think of being
old,) 'Don't let us discourage one another.'*

EDWARDS. *'Why, Doctor, you look stout and hearty, I am happy to see you so; for the newspapers told us you were very ill.'*

JOHNSON. *'Ay, Sir, they are always telling lies of US OLD FELLOWS.'*

*Wishing to be present at more of so singular a conversation as that between two fellow-collegians, who had lived forty years in London without ever having chanced to meet, I whispered to Mr. Edwards that Dr. Johnson was going home, and that he had better accompany him now. So Edwards walked along with us, I eagerly assisting to keep up the conversation. Mr. Edwards informed Dr. Johnson that he had practised long as a solicitor in Chancery, but that he now lived in the country upon a little farm, about sixty acres, just by Stevenage in Hertfordshire, and that he came to London (to Barnard's Inn, No. 6), generally twice a week. Johnson appearing to me in a reverie, Mr. Edwards addressed himself to me, and expatiated on the pleasure of living in the country.*

BOSWELL. '*I have no notion of this, Sir. What you have to entertain you, is, I think, exhausted in half an hour.*'

EDWARDS. '*What? Don't you love to have hope realized? I see my grass, and my corn, and my trees growing. Now, for instance, I am curious to see if this frost has not nipped my fruit-trees.*'

JOHNSON. *(Whom we did not imagine was attending,)* '*You find, Sir, you have fears as well as hopes.*'—*So well did he see the whole, when another saw but the half of a subject.*

*When we got to Dr. Johnson's house, and were seated in his library, the dialogue went on admirably.*

EDWARDS. '*Sir, I remember you would not let us say* PRODIGIOUS *at College. For even then, Sir, (turning to me,) he was delicate in language, and we all feared him.*'

JOHNSON. *(To Edwards,)* '*From your having practised the law long, Sir, I presume you must be rich.*'

EDWARDS. 'No, Sir; I got a good deal of money; but I had a number of poor relations to whom I gave a great part of it.'

JOHNSON. 'Sir, you have been rich in the most valuable sense of the word.'

EDWARDS. 'But I shall not die rich.'

JOHNSON. 'Nay, sure, Sir, it is better to LIVE rich than to DIE rich.'

EDWARDS. 'I wish I had continued at College.'

JOHNSON. 'Why do you wish that, Sir?'

EDWARDS. 'Because I think I should have had a much easier life than mine has been. I should have been a parson, and had a good living, like Bloxam and several others, and lived comfortably.'

JOHNSON. 'Sir, the life of a parson, of a conscientious clergyman, is not easy. I have always considered a clergyman as the father of a larger family than he is able to maintain. I would rather have Chancery suits upon my hands than the cure of souls. No, Sir, I do not

*envy a clergyman's life as an easy life, nor do I
envy the clergyman who makes it an easy life.'*

*Here taking himself up all of a sudden,
he exclaimed, 'O! Mr. Edwards! I'll convince
you that I recollect you. Do you remember
our drinking together at an alehouse near
Pembroke gate? At that time, you told me
of the Eton boy, who, when verses on our
SAVIOUR'S turning water into wine were
prescribed as an exercise, brought up a
single line, which was highly admired, "Vidit
et erubuit lympha pudica DEUM," and I
told you of another fine line in Camden's
Remains, an eulogy upon one of our Kings,
who was succeeded by his son, a prince
of equal merit: "Mira cano, Sol occubuit,
nox nulla secuta est."' [Johnson said to me
afterwards, 'Sir, they respected me for my
literature: and yet it was not great but by
comparison. Sir, it is amazing how little
literature there is in the world.'—BOSWELL]*

*EDWARDS. 'You are a philosopher, Dr.
Johnson. I have tried too in my time to
be a philosopher; but, I don't know how,*

*cheerfulness was always breaking in.'—Mr. Burke, Sir Joshua Reynolds, Mr. Courtenay, Mr. Malone, and, indeed, all the eminent men to whom I have mentioned this, have thought it an exquisite trait of character. The truth is, that philosophy, like religion, is too generally supposed to be hard and severe, at least so grave as to exclude all gaiety.*

*EDWARDS. 'I have been twice married, Doctor. You, I suppose, have never known what it was to have a wife.'*

*JOHNSON. 'Sir, I have known what it was to have a wife, and (in a solemn, tender, faltering tone) I have known what it was to LOSE A WIFE. It had almost broke my heart.'*

*EDWARDS. 'How do you live, Sir? For my part, I must have my regular meals, and a glass of good wine. I find I require it.'*

*JOHNSON. 'I now drink no wine, Sir. Early in life I drank wine: for many years I drank none. I then for some years drank a great deal.'*

EDWARDS. 'Some hogs-heads, I warrant you.'

JOHNSON. 'I then had a severe illness, and left it off, and I have never begun it again. I never felt any difference upon myself from eating one thing rather than another, nor from one kind of weather rather than another. There are people, I believe, who feel a difference; but I am not one of them. And as to regular meals, I have fasted from the Sunday's dinner to the Tuesday's dinner, without any inconvenience. I believe it is best to eat just as one is hungry: but a man who is in business, or a man who has a family, must have stated meals. I am a straggler. I may leave this town and go to Grand Cairo, without being missed here or observed there.'

EDWARDS. 'Don't you eat supper, Sir?'

JOHNSON. 'No, Sir.'

EDWARDS. 'For my part, now, I consider supper as a turnpike through which one must pass, in order to get to bed.'

JOHNSON. *'You are a lawyer, Mr. Edwards. Lawyers know life practically. A bookish man should always have them to converse with. They have what he wants.'*

EDWARDS. *'I am grown old: I am sixty-five.'*

JOHNSON. *'I shall be sixty-eight next birthday. Come, Sir, drink water, and put in for a hundred.'*

*This interview confirmed my opinion of Johnson's most humane and benevolent heart. His cordial and placid behaviour to an old fellow-collegian, a man so different from himself; and his telling him that he would go down to his farm and visit him, showed a kindness of disposition very rare at an advanced age. He observed, 'how wonderful it was that they had both been in London forty years, without having ever once met, and both walkers in the street too!' Mr. Edwards, when going away, again recurred to his consciousness of senility, and looking full in Johnson's face, said to him, 'You'll find in Dr. Young, "O my coevals! Remnants of yourselves."'*

*Johnson did not relish this at all; but shook his head with impatience. Edwards walked off, seemingly highly pleased with the honour of having been thus noticed by Dr. Johnson. When he was gone, I said to Johnson, I thought him but a weak man.*

*JOHNSON. 'Why, yes, Sir. Here is a man who has passed through life without experience: yet I would rather have him with me than a more sensible man who will not talk readily.* [2]

Here Dr. Johnson demonstrates a genial sense of curiosity about another man's life and furnishes some homespun philosophy about the virtues and acquired wisdoms that come with experience. When Boswell mentions that Edwards has a weak intellect, Johnson replies that he would rather converse with a man like Edwards, who will talk readily, than spend time with a man with a superior intellect who guards his language. This is the delight in mutual elevation that Plato and Cicero both endorsed, and which good conversation sustains. Johnson reminds us that conversation isn't a legal deposition or an academic

[2]  From the Gutenberg e-text of Boswell's "Life of Johnson."

debate or salesmanship. The term "kindness of disposition" is always central to this art.

One of the greatest conversations in film occurs in Louis Malle's 1981 movie *My Dinner with Andre,* starring Wallace Shawn and Andre Gregory. The movie takes place in a restaurant in New York City and Shawn and Gregory play two actors who talk about life in the theater, imagination, and the philosophical problem of knowing what reality truly is. Gregory's character has lived an adventurous life staging avant garde art experiments which include having had the experience of being buried alive. Shawn's character is a more pragmatic person who wonders about the extremism of living a life in the service of art for art's sake. The film is entirely devoted to their dinner conversation and conversation as we've already seen doesn't need a plot.

If you're looking to literature and film for a racier example of conversation there's no better example than Nicholson Baker's 1992 novel *Vox*. The novel places the reader in the position of eavesdropping. The reader is essentially a wiretapper hearing a man and a woman engage in phone sex.

In case you're tempted to dismiss this just let me add that *Vox* portrays a superb and philosophical conversation about the erotic joy of being alive and the book is both a classic of dialogue and a superior example of the simultaneous elevation of conversation.

Again, both the characters are surprised by the art of sharing language itself. And no one has to be the winner, which means of course that everybody wins.

# Do Not Interrupt

Who are the great conversationalists of history? The list is a long one, for men and women who take a sincere interest in their companions are not as rare as we would imagine. A list of great conversationalists would have to include:

* The ancient Chinese poet **Tu Fu**. He walked the remote mountains, visited friends, and would famously sit up all night and talk about the meaning of aging or of love or of loss. My favorite translations of this poet are by the American poet Kenneth Rexroth.

* **Jonathan Swift**. A founding member of the famous "Kit Kat Club" (not to be confused with contemporary striptease clubs), Swift was renowned for his witty and capacious talk with notable writers and painters, including Addison and Steele.

* **Lord Byron**. The greatest conversationalist of the Romantic Age. See the memoirs of Lady Blessington.

- **Lord Chesterfield**. Eighteenth-century British statesman and writer. He was admired by learned societies both in Britain and France. That's a high honor and a true recommendation that the man could listen as well as enliven.

- **Thomas Paine**. One of the key writers and conversationalists of the Enlightenment.

- **Thomas Jefferson**. Though our third president could be didactic, he was also genial and marked by curiosity and, according to legend, dining with the father of our independence was a convivial and thoughtful entertainment.

- A surprising choice perhaps: "Old Hickory," **President Andrew Jackson**. Though he was a rough-and-tumble figure who rose from the American frontier, he was an admirer of Chesterfield. And he prized excellent talk around his table.

- **Abraham Lincoln**. Our sixteenth president was a colorful storyteller but also a first-rate listener. It is unfortunate that after he won the presidency he never had time for dinner and casual talk. Yet all his friends from Illinois

remember his tremendous warmth and enthu-
siasm for conversation.

❖ This one is no surprise: **Mark Twain**. His
true conversational genius was most on dis-
play with children. He would play elaborate
talking games with his daughters.

❖ As already noted: **Alexander Graham Bell**.
Like many nineteenth-century Americans,
Bell believed that civic life depended on
conversation. Many people still don't know
that his invention of the telephone came
about because he was attempting to make
a machine that would help the hearing
impaired.

❖ **Sam Houston**. Never mind that he was the
governor of two states, a senator, the founding
father of Texas, and all that. Houston famously
went to live with the Cree Indians when he
was still a young man, and the Crees adopted
him into their tribe. Enough said?

❖ **Charles Dickens**. Comic and garrulous, he
knew how to talk in every social setting, a
talent that makes his writings immortal.

❖ **Elizabeth Cady Stanton**. Her conversation was dazzling and she inspired women on the long march toward voting rights.

❖ **Walt Whitman**. Genial, curious, always civic minded and engaging with old friends and new acquaintances. Much has been written about Whitman's reception of guests during his later years. See notably the work of Horace Traubel.

❖ **Frederick Douglass**. All accounts reveal that he was as brilliant in his talk as he was on paper or at the lectern.

❖ **Oscar Wilde**. I'd like to have been a fly on the wall when he talked with George Bernard Shaw.

❖ **Jane Addams**. Founder of Hull House, feminist, and peace activist. She was known for her warmth for others and a keen appreciation regarding what those around her had to say. Community is about conversation.

❖ **Gertrude Stein**. Poet, essayist, doyenne of the modernist avant-garde in the twentieth century, impresario of the "lost generation" that included Ernest Hemingway and F. Scott Fitzgerald, a close friend of Picasso, with her lover Alice B. Toklas a guiding spirit of gay literature, a civil rights activist—and yes, according to all, a beautiful conversationalist. Playful and unafraid of curiosity.

❖ **Helen Keller**. World traveler and founder of the American Foundation for the Blind, Keller spoke through her hands with everyone from Enrico Caruso to Maori chieftains.

❖ **Langston Hughes**. You can't create a Renaissance just by living on the page. A kind man who could share his heart and soul.

❖ **Franklin D. Roosevelt**. Some thought him altogether "too charming," but all who knew him best note that he was not only interested in others but he heard what they had to say. He was entirely equaled in the art of conversation by his able first lady, Eleanor Roosevelt, who thought everyone was important and backed that view in all her public work.

❖ **G. K. Chesterton**. Moderate in thought and manner, Chesterton was beloved by those on the left and the right. His brand of intellectual amusement is remembered in all accounts of this singular writer's life.

❖ **All railway conductors** throughout history. Alas their art only dimly survives in the United States.

❖ **Joseph Mitchell**. Longtime writer for the *New Yorker* magazine, author of the most interesting literary nonfiction in mid-twentieth-century American letters. He could draw conversation out of his subjects, which is more than half the tango.

❖ **Arthur M. Schlesinger, Jr.** Historian and close friend of President John F. Kennedy. Schlesinger was an uncommon academic, evincing respect and fascination for the lives of others.

❖ **Harper Lee**. Author of the novel *To Kill a Mockingbird*. Close friend of Truman Capote. Without her southern charm Capote wouldn't have been able to successfully interview the people of Holcomb, Kansas, for his best-selling book *In Cold Blood*.

❖ **Duke Ellington**. One of the world's great late-night conversationalists.

❖ **Paulo Freire**. Twentieth-century educator and writer. Unlike John Dewey (who discouraged the idea of equality in the classroom), Freire spent his life helping the poor and oppressed gain access to education. He saw conversation as the stepping-stone to owning the life of the mind.

❖ *Beyond the Fringe*. British comedy team, which premiered on television in the UK in 1961. The group included Peter Cook, Dudley Moore, Alan Bennett, and Dr. Jonathan Miller. The Fringe influenced successive teams of comic conversationalists, including The Beatles and Monty Python.

❖ Opera tenor **Placido Domingo**. Well known for his humane spirit.

❖ **Isaiah Berlin**. Twentieth-century philosopher and public intellectual. He counted among his friends everyone from Virginia Woolf to Winston Churchill, W. H. Auden to

Boris Pasternak. Berlin was a keen student of decency in all its forms.

- **Richard Feynman**. Physicist. "We can talk about mystery and awe. That's what we have in common."

- **Bill Russell**. NBA Hall of Fame basketball player and coach with the Boston Celtics. His conversations with everyone from Dick Gregory to Kevin Garnett are first-rate examples of wisdom and a humorous appreciation of what it means to be fully alive.

- **Pete Seeger**. Folk musician and environmentalist. Like his friend Woody Guthrie, Pete can talk to anyone.

- **Maya Angelou**. Poet. "I've learned that people will forget what you said, people will forget what you did, but people will never forget how you made them feel."

Certainly the list of conversationalists above is not exhaustive: it's merely a starting point for a "Great Conversationalists' Hall of Fame." What links these people is their affection for diversity and their sincere interest in marrying their thoughts to those of others. It's impossible to overstress just how much true conversation depends on the creation of a shared and genial feeling that's larger than the talk of one individual. As the Roman orator Keipo said, "Who is the happiest of men? He who values the merits of others and in their pleasures takes joy, even as though t'were his own."

# EPILOGUE

**Though this book** was designed to be a slim volume, I have constructed it around the largest of human themes, as joy is the soul of play. As Socrates tells us in the *Symposium,* all speculation about devotion and love represents our noblest gift to our friends and to our gods.

Another way to think of this joy is to conceive of conversing as a form of jazz in which two or more musicians share an improvisation. No one knows for certain where this exercise will wind up.

Word games like Botticelli or Apples to Apples are a fun way to get people talking around a table, but these are guessing games and they don't lead toward the sweetly unforeseeable surprise of conversation.

I remain in thrall to the Greeks. Call your friends together and ask them to sing the praises of love.

SILVER BAY PUBLIC LIBRARY

It isn't a debate.

Don't set up an argument. Avoid asking, "Who was the greatest first baseman of all time?" Try to stick to the speculative caves of making.

The poet Theodore Roethke (who is one of my favorite writers) once asked in one of his note-books, "What's winter for?" He answered his query this way: "To remember love."

What's winter for?

What's the greatest thing about childhood? Old age?

If you're not a sailor or a scientist what use are the stars?

Why is music the mother of memory?

Take notes just as Plato finally did.

Oh, and turn off your mobile phones.

# About the Author

**Stephen Kuusisto** attended Hobart and William Smith Colleges in Geneva, New York, and did his graduate work in the Writer's Workshop at the University of Iowa. He is the author of *Only Bread, Only Light,* a collection of poems from Copper Canyon Press, and of the memoirs *Planet of the Blind* (a *New York Times* Notable Book) and *Eavesdropping: A Memoir of Blindness and Listening.* His poems and essays have appeared in numerous magazines and journals including *Harper's,* the *New York Times,* the *Washington Post,* and *Reader's Digest.*

He holds a dual appointment at the University of Iowa, where he teaches in the creative nonfiction program, and in the University of Iowa's College of Medicine. He has appeared as a guest on *The Oprah Winfrey Show,* the Arts & Entertainment Network, National Public Radio, *Dateline,* and with his guide dog on *Animal Planet.* He hosts a blog entitled Planet of the Blind (http://www.planet-of-the-blind.com). He lives in Iowa City, Iowa, with his wife, Connie.

# Index

## A

## B

## C

# D

# E

# INDEX